Australia

The guide to your work and travel
adventure

John Engeln

"There are no foreign lands. It is the traveller only who is foreign."

— Robert Louis Stevenson

Table of Contents

CHAPTER 1: Introduction 10
   How to use this guide 10
   What 's special 10
   Facts... 11
   Dangerous animals.. 14
   Aussie slang 15

CHAPTER 2: Preparation.. 16
   Why should you go?....................................... 16
   How long should you go 17
   When to go 18
   Language skills... 19
   Flights.. 20
   Return Flight 21
   Visa... 21
   Insurance... 25
   Vaccination 26
   Driver's license 27
   Where to start 27
   Hostels.. 28
   Pre plan 28

CHAPTER 3: The flight 30
   What to pack.. 30
   Documents 32
   Baggage 33
   Airport etiquette 33
   When landed 35

CHAPTER 4: Down Under 37
   Mobile phones 37
   Internet in Australia... 38

Bank account 39
TFN 41
Weather 42
Water, food and beer Water 44
The metric system 46
Power 46
Shopping 47

CHAPTER 5: Travel 48
Accommodation 48
Travel agencies 54
What cities to see 55
Take a course 57
Travel routes 58
Nightlife 68
Getting around 69

CHAPTER 6: Work 74
What kind of work 74
Backpacking jobs 75
Cards and certificates 76
Resume basics 77
Skills 80
Average income 81
Best paying jobs 82
Where to find jobs 83
Jobs online 84
Seasonal harvest work 84

CHAPTER 7: Money 86
Living costs 86
Travel costs 87
Expensive things 87
A year in numbers 88
How to save money 89

Taxes 91
Tax return 92
Superannuation 93
Moving money 94

CHAPTER 8: The first week 96
Get started 96
What to do 97

CHAPTER 9: The first month 98
Travel plans 98
Work plans 99
Money plans 99
Don't be surprised 100

CHAPTER 10: Second year 101
How to qualify 101
How to get it 102

CHAPTER 11: Post Australia 103
Travel some more 103
Second year 105
Study 105
Work 105

CHAPTER 12: Links 107
General sites 107
Travel 108
Work 112
Money 113
Apps 116

G'day,

This guide was designed to show you how easy and cheap it can be to travel to Australia. Whether if you are a tourist looking for a short term adventure or a backpacker who wants to go all in and Work & Travel for many months. Everything you need to know is explained in this book. From the preparation over the first weeks to what to do when you come back. This guide will get you started for the adventure of a lifetime. Even if you haven't made up your mind about a trip to Australia, the following pages might inspire you.

All the knowledge and experiences described in this book happened to me first hand and might paint a different picture compared to other people, but this is exactly the point - no two journeys are alike.
Just jump in a have an awesome adventure.

CHAPTER 1: Introduction

This chapter will show you what is so special about Australia, things you definitely should know before traveling there and how you can use this book to your advantage.

How to use this guide

The best way is to read the whole thing from start to finish. Or jump directly to the chapters you're most interested in. After a while you should not need this book anymore, but until then:

Have this book with you!

What 's special

Australia is famous for many things and it deserves them all. The People are the friendliest I have ever met, they're nice, really, really nice. From People that offer you a bed to sleep in, to people in a store that talk to you because they're genuinely interested in other human beings. Spending time in Australia will drastically improve your people skills and will destroy a lot of your prejudices.

Use these chances.

Australia is one of the few countries left, that has that special thing that can't be measured nor explained. It will make you feel happy and satisfied for almost the whole journey. You will feel a sense of possibility, do things there you couldn't do anywhere else in the world.

Facts

Size
Australia is a continent and a country at once. With a size of more than 7.6 million square km it is the 6th largest country in the world. Still the population is just 23 million people. Of whom 95% live in close proximity to the coast. It is split into 7 states - Tasmania, New South Wales (NSW), Queensland (QLD), South Australia (SA), Northern Territory (NT) and Western Australia (WA).
The Australian capital is Canberra which is located in the Australian Capital Territory (ACT).

History
The first British settlement was established in the late

18th century. Before that it was only inhabited by indigenous Australians - Aborigines. The people and culture is still alive today and it's definitely worth visiting an indigenous centre and immersing oneself into Australia's past.

Since the colonial days a lot has changed. What started out as the biggest prison in history is now one of the richest countries in the world. Not just rich in money, but in culture, history, nature and people. Australia is as much a 21st century country as Japan, America or Europe and in some regards it is even more advanced.

Currency

The currency is the Australian Dollar. Rates vary but the general rule of thumb is that the Australian dollar is roughly 75% of the Euro and 80% of the US$.

- AUD$1 = 0,71 Euro
- AUD$1 = $0.78 US

Always be up to date on the rates when transferring money to Australia or vice versa.

Time Zones

Due to its size, Australia has multiple time zones.
The time difference between Sydney and Perth, for example, is 2 hours.

UTC - Universal Coordinate Time:

- Australian Central Daylight Time - UTC +10:30
- Australian Central Standard Time - UTC +9:30

Meaning 3:00pm in Sydney is 7.00 am in Frankfurt, Germany and 01:00 am in New York City, USA.

Climate

The climate varies a lot dependent on the region you. The largest part of the country is desert or dry land. Only in proximity to the ocean you will find a balanced climate. The North is mostly tropical and has rain forests and grasslands. Australia is in the southern hemisphere and the seasons are inverted. If you're from the northern hemisphere, which you most likely are, and leave in summer you will arrive in the Australian winter, which means still good weather and warm temperatures in most parts.

The overall climate is quite warm and sunny.

The 5 largest cities in Australia by population are:
- Sydney with 4,9 million
- Melbourne with 4,5 million
- Brisbane with 2,3 million
- Perth with 2 million
- Adelaide with 1,3 million

Dangerous animals

There is one common misconception that I want to clear up right away and it is about dangerous animals. Many people I talk to, are afraid of going to Australia because of it. Let's give it some truth.

YES - there are many dangerous animals in Australia.

NO - you most likely will not encounter them.

Because they are not crawling around in every corner. These animals are hiding and are afraid of humans. In all my time there I saw maybe 5 or 6 snakes and spiders, that's it. And I worked in very remote locations. Chances are that you will never see one dangerous animal, not one. It is more likely to get run over by a car.

If, against all odds, you encounter a snake or something similar, it is best to keep calm and move away very slowly. If you're bitten, rush to the next hospital ASAP. They are prepared for occasions like this and can help you.

Aussie slang

Here are a few commonly used phrases, that might help you understand the Australians a bit better.

No worries!	-	No problem
G'day!	-	Hello!
Joey	-	Baby kangaroo
Jackaroo	-	Male station hand
Jillaroo	-	Female station hand
Maccas	-	McDonalds
Mate	-	Mate
Mozzie	-	Mosquito
Oz	-	Australia
Paddock	-	Field
Pommy	-	Someone from England
Sunnies	-	Sunglasses
Piss	-	Beer
Tea	-	Supper
Ute	-	Utility vehicle
Vedgies	-	Vegetables
Aussie	-	Australian
Ace!	-	Very good!
Bloke	-	Guy
Bottle shop	-	Liquor store
Brizzie	-	Brisbane
Bush	-	Outback
Chook	-	Chicken
Esky	-	insulated food container

CHAPTER 2: Preparation

Why should you go?

You might finish school in a few months, you're done with university or you are just bored by your 9 to 5 job. These are reasons to go and to have an extraordinary trip. When I first played with the idea to go to Australia it was more like an excuse to tell everyone who was asking about my future. It took me 3 months to turn this vague idea into a real plan and to execute it. At first I was afraid of everything, the long distance from home (16.000 km), the language and the people.

I preferred sitting at home and walking in beaten paths, but the more I thought about it the more I liked the idea of doing something new and unknown.

Australia was the best and most rewarding experience in my life, yes there might be other things in the future but I doubt that they will be as good.

This trip changed my view about the world, about people and about everything else. Each day was a rewarding adventure with one primary goal - doing what you want to do. It forged me into a new person with no fear about doing my own thing and being independent. If you would ask me if you should go, I'd say, "Hell Yeah" this is your opportunity to do something great. Don't think about it, just do it.

I took the chance and left for more than 2,5 years.

How long should you go

It depends on your plans, if you begin university, have another job lined up after your trip or just need a vacation you probably will have a limited timeframe.

When on Vacation:
- 2 weeks is too short as it takes you 4 days only to get there and back.
- 4 weeks is a good start but,
- 6 weeks or more is recommended to actually see some things.

When on a Working Holiday Visa:
- 4 months is almost too short,
- 6 months is a start for most people, but
- 12 months or more are recommended to experience everything.

My suggestion is to do 12 months. It is easy to get carried away when traveling and time goes faster as you think. Also once the visa is activated you never get the time back when leaving earlier.

If you can't get enough of it, you can qualify for a 2nd Year Visa which allows you to stay an additional 12 months, more on that later. But you might love it so much that you want stay forever, easy enough, a friend of mine did just that. All you need is an employer who is willing to sponsor you for three to four years and then you're eligible for an Australian citizenship. But don't get carried away, there might be a great life waiting for you outside Australia.

This is a once in a lifetime chance.

When to go

The best time to go to Australia is the late summer, between June and September (in the northern hemisphere). The weather and temperatures are nice and spring is just around the corner in the southern hemisphere. Students who finish school in summer do it usually like this. If you're a person who likes it a bit more quite, you should probably go earlier or later. But if you want to meet many new friends from all around the world, summer is your time.

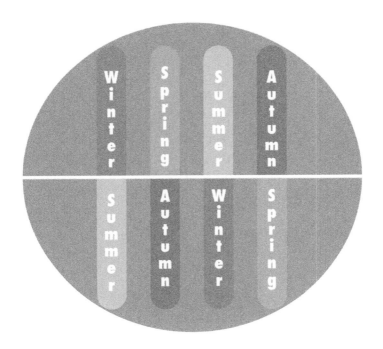

Language skills

If you're a native English speaker you're good to go. When English is your second language and you're insecure or think your skills are not sufficient enough, it makes sense to take a language course. They can be taken in your home country or in Australia. But keep in mind, you learn much more by just speaking a language, don't be afraid, just jump right in, immerse yourself. Also, you're reading this book, meaning you know English.

Flights

The probably only way to get to Australia in a timely manner is by plane. Just keep an eye on cheap flight over a month, compare different airlines and travel sites. Also become a frequent flyer member, all the miles you will earn will allow you to buy something cool in the end, like a hotel stay or an upgraded flight. 6.000 miles for one way from Frankfurt to Sydney are common.

Recommended Airlines:
- Emirates - www.emirates.com
- Qantas - www.qantas.com.au

they offer excellent service, an average price and fast transit times and have joined routes.

Duration
A flight takes on average 24 hours, from Europe, with one stopover in Dubai. From New York City it takes roughly the same time, flying the other way around the planet with one stopover in Los Angeles.

Prices
1300 Euro (US$1500) for a return flight from Europe or the USA are common and one way trips can be bought from 600 Euro (US$700) to 800 Euro (US$900) a piece.

Return Flight

The visa requirements specify that you must hold a return flight, but airlines make flights only available 335 days in advance. Meaning if you stay longer, you have to reschedule your return flight, which will cost between AU$180 and AU$230. In practice it's almost never checked upon entry but don't challenge your luck.

When booking a flight, try to find one that arrives at night (Australian time) so you can check in and go to bed right after landing and get up in the morning to work against the jet leg.

Visa

In order to get to Australia, you need to have a valid passport. Chances are you have one but if not, apply for one as soon as possible and make sure it is valid for the whole time you're in the country.

Check the Australian Immigration Department for more information: www.border.gov.au

As a Tourist

There are 3 types of tourist visas, for all of them you have to be outside Australia when applying. Different countries require different visas, for example if you're from the United States you need to apply for an Electronic Travel Authority, if you're from Germany you need to apply for an eVisitor visa. To find out what kind of visa you need, go to the Australian immigration office online: www.border.gov.au/Trav/Visi/Visi

Electronic Travel Authority (subclass 601) - visit Australia for business and travel purposes, as many times as you want for a whole year and a stay for up to 3 months for each visit. Costs: AU$20

eVisitor (subclass 651) - visit Australia for business and travel purposes, for up to 3 months at a time within a 12 months' period. Costs: FREE

Visitor Visa (subclass 600) - visit for business and travel purposes, for up to 3, 6 or 12 months. Costs: from AU$130 to AU$335

Work & Travel

Visa requirements: Your age is between 18 and 31,

valid passport, AU$5000, return flight and health insurance for the duration of your stay.

Working Holiday Visa (subclass 417) - lets you work and travel within Australia for up to 12 months. You can work for up to 6 months for each employer. Study for 3 months, leave and re-enter Australia as many times you like during the visa period.

- The official Visa site: www.border.gov.au/Trav/Visa-1/417-

First Visa: You must be outside Australia during application and when it is granted.

Costs: AU$440 online, paper form AU$520.

Second Year Visa: You can be in Australia when you apply, you also must be in Australia when it is granted or you apply from outside Australia then you must be outside of Australia when it is granted.

Costs: AU$440 online, paper form AU$520.

- Visa Pricing estimator www.border.gov.au/Trav/Visa/Visa-1

Work and Holiday Visa (subclass 462) - lets you work and travel within Australia for up to 12 months. You can work for up to 6 months for each employer. Study for 3 months, leave and re-enter Australia as many times you like during the visa period.

There is a limit for first 462 visas for each country each year, once this limit is reached no applications will be approved.

Costs: AU$440 online.

- For further information visit this link: www.border.gov.au/Trav/Visa-1/462-

Make sure to check your exact visa requirements.

The AU$5000

It is required to have at least AU$5000 (3500 Euro or US$3900) to get you started in Australia. But no one controls it, I know people who arrived with only AU$400 in their pockets and made it somehow. You need a bank statement, with you as the account owner and the amount available, no older than 2 weeks. I still recommend this amount of money. It gives you a cushion and the chance to travel and relax first and look for a job later. Your parents can transfer the money to your account and you transfer it back to them after you printed the statement. But if you only have AU$2000 you can still do it. Wages are very high in Australia and if you do it right you can save a lot of money, even beyond your time in Australia.

Application Process

The online application process takes between 15 and 20 minutes, all you need is your passport and a credit card. It is straight forward and easy to complete. When applying for the first time, it usually only takes two hours to get the visa confirmation via e-mail.

Insurance

Health insurance

While traveling in Australia, you're required to have a valid health insurance. There are special insurance packages available for people who do Work & Holiday trips, they range from two months to 24 months and are very easy to extend should your trip take longer. They're about 65 Euros (US$70) per month, which totals 780 Euro (US$840) a year. If you plan to travel to other countries after your Australian adventure, make sure that your insurance covers them as well.

Insurance companies:

- Allianz with Elvia Overseas Protection
  http://www.allianz-assistance.co.uk
- CareMed - https://www.work-and-travel-insurance.com

Many more offers can be found online, but make sure to ask your current health insurance company. They might offer such a service, which could save some money. If you are in Australia just for a few weeks on vacation, just make sure to have a standard travel insurance. It is never, seriously never, a good idea to travel without insurance. When you get sick and have to go to the doctor or hospital, it can be ridiculously expensive and you don't want to break the bank.
Serious injuries that require long hospital treatments

might require you to return to your country, most insurance companies fly you home for proper treatment, but make sure to check.

Other Insurances
Consider the following insurances as well. They are not a requirement but usually a good idea.
- Liability Insurance - if you break it you don't have to for pay it.
- Insurance cover - if you can't make the journey in the first place, this will get you your money back.
- Luggage Insurance - if your bag is lost or stolen, you get at least the value back.

Some health insurance companies offer the services mentioned above in addition to your health insurance for little extra money.

Vaccination

Make sure to check with your doctor before you go, and refresh your routine vaccines if required. Make a routine health check anyway before leaving. When traveling to other countries afterwards make sure to check their vaccination requirements.

For Australia, no special vaccination is required.

Driver's license

If you have a normal driver's license, in this example an EU license, you just go to the "administrative district office" or the authority that issued your license and they will provide an International License. It takes roughly 15 minutes and costs around 15 Euros. This license allows you to drive in almost any country on earth and is valid for three years. Additionally, you need to have your original license with you in order to drive.

If you don't have a driver's license, it might be an option to acquire one in Australia. They are much cheaper as in most European countries and take less time. But before beginning with a license in Australia, make sure to check with your local authorities if it is possible to transfer it.

Australians drive on the left side of the road.

Where to start

You might not know from where to start, if you have never been to Australia. The following cities are common for tourists and backpackers alike:
- Sydney
- Brisbane
- Perth
- Melbourne

If you are not sure, I suggest you start in Sydney, the

biggest and probably best city in Australia. Everybody knows Sydney and there is a ton of cool stuff to see and do. Of course you also can start in any other city but flights might not be as frequent or cheap. Check multiple cities before booking a flight.

Hostels

The flight to the city of your choice is booked. Now it is time to take care of some accommodation for the first few days, because no one wants to look for a place to sleep after a 24h flight. Hostels are a cheap and great way to spend the night. The rooms are available as single or multi bed rooms usually for 4 - 6 people. They're priced quite reasonable and are used mostly by people like you, backpackers or budget tourists from all over the world. Costs range from AU$25 to AU$45 per night for a 4 - 6 bed dorm. If you're looking for something more luxurious you can take a hotel, they start around AU$100 per night in big cities.

It's the perfect way to make new friends and get started.

Pre plan

When arriving in Australia and getting everything sorted (CHAPTER 4: Down Under), it takes a while for them to arrive. A bank card takes 2 - 3 weeks and your tax file number 28 days. Plan the first few weeks of your journey in advance so the mail is sent to the appropriate place. You can use the hostel address where you will be staying in a month from your application date and pick up your mail there. After the 1st month you should have all your papers and should be able to make more spontaneous plans. If you're in Australia just for vacation this doesn't concern you.

Hostels receive a lot of mail and you can receive it without staying there.

CHAPTER 3: The flight

There are just a few more things you have to do before you can begin your journey. These things are listed here.

What to pack

Attention!
- Knifes, scissors and sharp objects are not allowed in your carry-on luggage.
- Don't bring your best clothes as the they get ruined while travelling.

The checklist below is a rough outline of what you should pack:
- Passport
- Visa (copy of your e-mail confirmation)
- Hostel / Hotel booking confirmation
- Address or route to your Hostel / Hotel
- Drivers Licence (International and your original)
- Medial ID (your blood type, allergies, etc.)

- Travel pharmacy
- First Aid Travel Kit
- Insurance documents
- Important certificates
- Credit card and debit card
- About AU$500 in cash (for the first few days)
- Bank statement with AU$5000
- Your smartphone
- Laptop or tablet
- Sunglasses
- Sun protection (30+)
- Headphones
- Flip Flops
- Sturdy shoes
- Small lock
- Pen and paper
- Power adapter
- Pocket knife
- Clothes
- Raincoat

Remember, everything you pack you have to carry.

Documents

It is a good idea to bring important documents and to keep multiple copies. Save them on your smartphone and in the cloud or in your email account, so you can access them anywhere anytime.

Cloud Services you can use for a backup:
- Google Drive - https://www.google.com.au/drive/ (15 GB)
- Drop Box - www.dropbox.com (up to 6GB)

These services also allow easy photo sharing with friends and family.

Bring the following documents and keep copies of them:
- Passport
- Driver's License
- International Driver's License
- Degrees (school, university, work)
- Certificates
- Insurance Policy
- Credit and debit cards

If you have any of the following things, also make copies of them:
- Additional Licenses (Boat, Truck, Forklift, etc.)
- anything else that has value to you.

Baggage

Checked baggage is usually included in your flight, but check beforehand. The weight can range from 23kg to 32kg for one bag. Make sure to pack your suitcase at least 3 days prior to departure and check the weight at home. Paying for overweight at the airport is very expensive.

Australia is one of the best developed nations on earth, so forget about the outback and dirt roads that everybody is thinking about. They have paved roads and top notch transportation. A backpack is easy to carry and good for walking a lot, but it can only carry up to 70 litres. On the other hand a suitcase can carry much heavier loads but needs flat terrain.

It is up to you and your preferences, when I arrived in Australia with a backpack I quickly realised that a suitcase would suit me more - pun not intended.

Airport etiquette

This might be the first time you fly, or at least for that long. Here are 11 simple rules to follow which will make your airport experience a blessing.

1. Dress comfortably for your flight.

2. Arrive at least three hours in advance. When heading to Australia it is possible that a lot of people will be on your plane and there will be a long

line at the counter of your airline. Just arrive early to beat that line or use a check in kiosk.

3. Have your baggage prepared at home, don't start packing at the airport. Also don't put batteries in your checked baggage, they are carry on. Make sure your suitcase is not too heavy.

4. Have your passport ready for check in. Check in usually opens three hours before flight.

5. Make sure you change your euros, dollars, pounds, etc. into Australian dollars, it's easy to do at the airport.

6. After check in, proceed to the security check and enter the departure area. Don't roam around the airport like it's a theme park. When approaching security check, you have to say goodbye to your friends and family.

7. Take off all metal chains, watches and belts and put them into the provided boxes, also remove your laptop / tablet from your bag and put it into an extra box during security screening.

8. After security check, grab your stuff and leave the area to make space for other people, don't get dressed right there.

9. Make sure to proceed to your gate in time. Boarding begins anyway, with or without you.

10. Listen to speaker announcements, planes are boarded in an order and if your seat row is not called, don't get in line.

11. When on the plane, find your seat, stow your bag, buckle up and have a nice flight.

When landed

You finally made it. Welcome to Australia.
All you have to do now is to go to border protection and immigrate into the country. Have your passport and the immigration card (the one you got on the plane) ready. Immigration is usually slow and takes forever, be patient. After all this is done you can go and pick up your bag. Leave the airport and head to your hostel or hotel.

There are multiple ways to get to your destination:
- Train
- Airport Shuttle Bus
- Taxi

The train is usually the fastest and cheapest one to use. Shuttle buses require pre booking and taxis are very expensive in Australia. If you arrive early at your hostel be prepared to wait, but usually you can drop your bags and go for a walk.

Most hostels and hotels let you check in after 2.00 pm.

CHAPTER 4: Down Under

The adventure can finally begin. This chapter will guide you through the important things to do after your arrival.

Mobile phones

With no constant address and always on the move, your phone and mobile internet are probably the most important tools in your travel bag. Having an Australian sim card makes sense for tourists and backpackers alike. Make sure that your smartphone is unlocked and accepts sim cards from different providers and can be used overseas.

The 4 largest carriers in Australia are:
- Telstra - www.telstra.com.au
- Optus - www.optus.com.au
- Vodafone - www.vodafone.com.au
- Virgin Mobile - www.virginmobile.com.au

Due to the small number of people in Australia the internet speeds over 3G and 4G are terrific. The fastest and most reliable carrier is Telstra, it is a bit more expensive but offers reception almost everywhere. This is crucial when on a road trip, working on a farm or otherwise being in a remote location. Sim cards are available in every Telstra branch and in grocery stores, news agencies and gas stations. The plain card can be bought for AU$2. A ready to go pre-paid card costs around AU$30.

I recommend to go into a branch and talk to a professional. They can activate your sim card immediately and set up your phone.

The second most reliable carrier is Optus, cheaper than Telstra and still with wide coverage. Depending on the options you choose on your sim card plan, calls cost around ¢10 - ¢15 for national and international calls. Oversea calls are cheap from within Australia and allow you to just call your friends and family at home. Make sure to get plenty of mobile data, at least 1GB per month.

For sufficient mobile coverage, choose Telstra!

Internet in Australia

Internet is available almost everywhere but most times it is limited, slow or costs money.

These places offer free Wi-Fi:
- McDonalds
- Hungry Jacks (Burger King)
- Libraries
- Public Spaces
- Train Stations
- Trains
- Cafes
- Stores
- Shopping Malls

Hostels and Hotels offer Wi-Fi for a charge which can be quite expensive. The advantage is that the Wi-Fi is unlimited and allows large data transfers for all YouTube lovers out there. Hostel Wi-Fi however is often slow due to many simultaneous users. If you want more independence and don't need unlimited data, you can use your phone as internet device or as a mobile hotspot. It also can make sense to by a mobile 3G / 4G Wi-Fi hotspot which uses a sim card to connect to the internet. This kind of internet is very fast and can supply multiple devices.

Time has shown that you get more data for the same money year by year. Telstra currently gives you 8GB of data for AU$50.

Bank account

One of the first things to do, after you got your sim card,

...nk account.

- Commonwealth Bank - www.commbank.com.au
- Westpac Bank - www.westpac.com.au
- Australian and New Zealand Banking - ANZ - www.anz.com.au
- National Australian Bank - NAB - www.nab.com.au

Out of my own experience I recommend the Commonwealth Bank, they have branches in almost every town and are the most reliable bank. Just walk into a branch and they will gladly assist you. Tellers in Australia are among the friendliest in the world. What you need is a "Complete Access Account", but also ask for a "Netbank Saver Account" which will give you interest on your money, currently 2,5% annually. Opening an account takes no longer than five minutes. Your debit card will be sent to the address you provide, most likely the one of your hostel.

If you're under the age of 21, the account is free until you reach that age, after that it is just AU$6 a month.

The card you receive is a Master Card debit card - it works like a credit card, you just can't go into debt. Be prepared to manage your account almost entirely online. When it comes to banking Australia is very advanced and almost everything is done over the internet. When opened, you can immediately deposit money into your new account. Without a card you can withdraw money only in a branch with your passport, it is cumbersome but possible. You can also set up a superannuation fund during your bank visit, which is required if you want to work.

Your card takes between 2-3 weeks.

TFN

The Tax File Number or TFN for short, allows you to get a legitimate job and to pay taxes. This number is required for everyone who wants to work in Australia, without it you, can't work, legally.

In order to apply for a TFN you need:
- A Work and Holiday Visa or any other kind of work visa,
- To be in Australia,
- A mail address within the country,
- Your passport,
- An e-mail address,
- A phone number.

For the application you can use your hostel address. Hostels always have a mailbox for their guests. Make sure to check it daily.

Further information is available here:
- Australian Taxation Office (ATO) -

www.ato.gov.au

- Information - www.ato.gov.au/individuals/tax-file-number/apply-for-a-tfn/foreign-passport-holders,-permanent-migrants-and-temporary-visitors---tfn-application/
- To apply for your TFN go to this page - https://iar.ato.gov.au/IARWeb/default.aspx?pid=4&sid=1&outcome=1

The application checks your visa status, make sure to provide valid information. Applying for a TFN is straight forward and takes between 15 and 20 minutes.

It takes up to 28 days before receiving the TFN via mail.

Weather

Australia is one of the driest countries in the world and every drop of water is worth saving.

Temperatures can range from negative temperatures in winter to 45 degrees Celsius or higher in summer, depending on your location. Along the coast the temperatures are balanced by the ocean and stay constant, meaning when you just came from the outback with frost at night, a night at the coast will be around 22 degrees. Make sure to pack or buy warm clothes when going into the country during winter. The sun is very intense and is shining almost all the time. Average sun hours per day are listed in the diagram below.

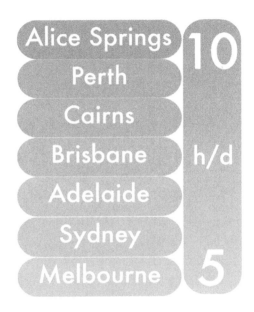

Alice Springs
Perth
Cairns
Brisbane
Adelaide
Sydney
Melbourne

10
h/d
5

Your skin can be burned quickly and more lasting. Just 20 minutes of noon sun is dangerous. Try to stay out of it during the most extreme times. Most hostels offer free sun protection at the counter, but always have your own. 30+ is good but 50 is the better choice.

Wear a hat when going outside and stay hydrated, this can mean drinking between one and ten litres of water a day, depending on your activity. There are drinking fountains almost everywhere.

Always use sun protection!

Some regions are subject to thunderstorms and floods

and can render roads unusable and dangerous. When caught in such a situation sit it out and don't try to drive through it.

And yes, there is snow in some parts of the country and if you're skiing this might be great for you. For more specific weather information use a weather service and check out the Australian Bureau of Meteorology: www.bom.gov.au

Water, food and beer Water

If you're from Europe you're used to drink form the tap. Not in Australia. The water is sterilised with chlorine, which is not meant to be drank over long periods of time. But for washing and cooking it's fine. In order to drink water, either use a filtration system, many hostels and private homes have one or buy bottled water in a store. If you work somewhere remote where it doesn't make sense to buy large quantities of water you can usually drink the water from the tab, or tank - ask your employer.

Food

For your survival you need a bit more than just water, food for example. There is plenty of it and you can get it very cheap when doing it right. The variety of food sold in Australia is the same as in the US and Europe. Due to the high living standards, it is also more expensive. Especially chocolate and imported things. All large chains offer off brand products that are cheaper and still have a decent quality. Also look out for discounts, "Buy 1 get 2", "50% off" etc. Discounts are available almost all the time and in almost any store.

The three major Supermarket chains are:
- Coles
- Woolworth
- Aldi

Local Supermarket chains are:
- IGA
- Foodworks
- Spar

Beer

Australian Beer and Australians belong together like water and life. Most beers are brewed in the country and if you don't want to show that you're a foreigner right away, drink an Australian brand. Imported beers are more expensive and harder to come by anyway. Alcohol in general is very expensive due to the high taxes, but no one cares and happily pays AU$50 for a carton of 24 bottles.

The four most common brands are:
- XXXX
- Carlton
- Tooheys

- VB

The metric system

For all people from Myanmar (Burma), Liberia and the United States, Australia is using the metric system, like the rest of world.

The chart shows the conversion rates:

1 ′	=	2.54 cm
1 ft	=	0.30 m
1 mi	=	1.6 km
1 gal	=	3.78 l
1 lb	=	0.45 kg

$$°C = (°F - 32) \times 5/9$$

Power

Go and get a power adapter before you start your journey, they can be bought in almost any electronic store or at the airport. Australia has special outlets with a switch, as seen below. The power grid runs on 230V and 50Hz, like most countries.

Exceptions are the US, Canada and Japan. They run on 100 / 120 V with 50 or 60 Hz. If you're from one of these countries check your power bricks if they can run on higher voltages.

Shopping

You find all the usual chains and giant malls in any larger city. Stores range from discounters like Target to supreme stores like Gucci, Ferrari and Apple. The small and local owned and manufactured goods are something you should focus on. You can't buy them anywhere else in the world and they make great gifts, from Australian made shirts and boots to Didgeridoos.

Many stores sell working clothes, boots and accessories for farming, mining and construction jobs that are required when working in such an environment.

If you plan on camping during your trip, buy your equipment in the country, it is cheap and can be found in almost any store. This saves you from packing a tent or sleeping bag into your luggage.

If you need something try www.ebay.com.au there is no Amazon just yet.

CHAPTER 5: Travel

You came to Australia to see something. This chapter will help you with the basics and gives you an overview.

Accommodation

Hostels

For you as a backpacker or budget traveller hostels are probably the most common way of staying somewhere. They are everywhere in almost every town, offer low prices and have a wide variety of facilities to accommodate your traveling needs. Hostels are the core ingredient of the backpacking lifestyle and you will always meet new and awesome people from all over the world with whom you might travel or have an adventure.

The two major Australian hostel chains are:
- YHA Australia - www.yha.com.au
- Nomads Backpackers - www.nomadsworld.com

They have branches in every larger city and you can

pre book and pay your next hostel in advance, other services also include a travel agency and a job board. Sometimes smaller hostels that don't belong to large chains offer better deals, look for them as well.

Facilities offered in hostels:
- TV and movie room
- Breakfast option
- Laundry
- Wi-Fi
- Internet computers
- Library
- Postal service
- Kitchen
- Cutlery and dishes
- Events and get-togethers

Dorm sizes range from 1-32 people. A 4-6 bed room is a good way to get started.

The less privacy you need the cheaper it gets.

Make sure to book your hostel in advance and keep an eye on public holidays or sport events which usually means that hostels are fully booked.
Calling the hostel and confirming your booking 24h prior to arrival is also recommended.

For starters, here are three good Hostels per City:
Sydney

- Sydney Central YHA - from AU$39 a night - https://www.yha.com.au/hostels/nsw/sydney-surrounds/sydney-central-backpackers-hostel/
- Blue Elephant - from AU$ 23 a night - http://www.elephantbackpacker.com.au
- Bounce Sydney - from AU$42 a night - http://www.bouncehostel.com.au

Brisbane

- Brisbane City YHA - from AU$25 a night - https://www.yha.com.au/hostels/qld/brisbane-surrounds/brisbane-backpackers-hostel/
- Chill Backpackers - from AU$29 a night - http://www.chillbackpackers.com
- X Base - from AU$23 a night - http://www.stayatbase.com/hostels/australia/brisbane/base-brisbane-uptown

Melbourne

- Melbourne Central YHA - from AU$36 a night - https://www.yha.com.au/hostels/vic/melbourne-hostels/melbourne-central-hostel/
- Nomads Melbourne - from AU$31 a night - http://nomadsworld.com/hostels/australia/melbourne/nomads-melbourne
- King Street Backpackers - from AU$30 a night http://www.kingstreetbackpackers.com.au

Cairns

- Cairns Central YHA - from AU$25 a night - https://www.yha.com.au/hostels/qld/cairns-and-far-north-queensland/cairns-backpackers-hostel/
- Nomads Cairns - from AU$16 a night - http://nomadsworld.com/hostels/australia/cairns/nomads-cairns
- Gilligans - from AU$24 a night - https://www.gilligans.com.au

Adelaide

- Adelaide Central YHA - from AU$30 a night - https://www.yha.com.au/hostels/sa/adelaide/adelaide-backpackers-hostel/
- Adelaide Travellers In - from AU$26 a night - http://nomadsworld.com/hostels/australia/adelaide/adelaide-travellers-inn
- Hostel 109 - from AU$32 a night - http://www.hostel109.com/

Perth

- Perth City YHA - from AU$29 a night - https://www.yha.com.au/hostels/wa/perth-surrounds/perth-backpackers-hostel/
- Billabong Backpackers - from AU$20 a night - http://nomadsworld.com/hostels/australia/perth/billabong-backpackers
- City Perth Backpackers Hostel - from AU$24 a night - http://www.cityperthhostel.com.au/rooms/

Hotels

Hotels are fairly expensive in Australia and just make sense for short term stays or special occasions. But after all your travels throughout Australia it might be time to calm down for a few days before returning home and sometimes you just need your own room to sleep in. Prices range from AU$30 in rural pubs to a couple AU$100 in high class city hotels. Australia has all the famous chains like Hilton, Four Seasons, Best Western, Rydges, Shangri-La and so on. Make sure to check sites like TripAdvisor from to time to time to see when prices drop.

Airbnb - www.airbnb.com.au

Another alternative that emerged over the past few years, is the use of Air Bed and Breakfast or short Airbnb.

This service gives people the chance to rent out their spare room for some money. The prices are reasonable and it is a great way to meet new people and to mingle with the locals. Airbnb is available in 190 countries and in any big city in Australia. It offers discounts for long term stays, from weekly prices to monthly prices. If you're not in the mood for a hostel and can't afford a hotel this is the way to go. The hosts are very friendly and will give you important information about their city and neighbourhood.

Apartments

Apartments are a great opportunity to save money and stay long term. It is possible to rent your own apartment or rent a room in a shared apartment with other people. When working in a city long time, this is more practical than living in a hostel, as you save money and have your privacy. Rental agreements can range from 1 - 6+ months, depending on the landlord. Shared apartments start from AU$200 per week.

If you have the necessary change, renting an apartment on the beach, be it just for a couple of days to enjoy a luxurious life style is also a sweet idea.

Friends and Australians

When having relatives or friends in Australia this might be a good way to save money and stay with them for a while.

Don't know anyone? No problem, you will meet a lot of new people and Australians have a very friendly nature, meaning someone you just met might offer you to stay with him for a few days - this is normal don't be afraid.

Camping

Camping is another way to save money and to experience some nature. Champing sites are very cheap or sometimes free. The paid ones usually offer Wi-Fi, showers and power. The free ones are mostly just large paddocks with a toilet somewhere. There are no camping sites in cities so you have to travel a fair bit, but when working rurally and you need a place to crush this might be a good option.

- Family Parks offers paid campsites in Australia and New Zealand www.familyparks.com.au
- Camping Australia lists almost all FREE campsites in Australia www.campinaustralia.com.au

Camper Van

Renting a Camper Van or a car is a great way to see the country and to save money on accommodation. Camper Vans are usually for 2 - 6 people. Just split the rental price and gas money.

You can rent vans from companies like:

- Jucy - www.jucy.com.au
- Wicked Campers - www.wickedcampers.com.au
- Hippie Camper- www.hippiecamper.com

When planning a long road trip you, it can make sense to buy your own car or camper van. There are plenty of them available from other backpackers and used car companies. Look at the black board in your hostel or at **www.gumtree.com.au.** Just make sure you get what you pay for, fraud and faulty vehicles are common.

Travel agencies

If you want to take a tour or trip somewhere, Travel

Agencies will help you out. In big cities you can find many different ones which are all located in the same area, usually. They offer services like free Wi-Fi, computers and of course travel information and booking.

Some of the big travel agencies are:
- Peterpans - www.peterpans.com.au
- YHA Travel - www.yha.com.au/travel-and-tours/tours-and-activities/
- Wicked Travel - www.wickedtravel.com.au

These agencies help you with booking single trips or whole itineraries and can get you cheap prices and discounts. Some even help you in finding a job.

What cities to see

Australia has just a hand full of large cities, but all with beautiful and diverse characters. This list contains the biggest and best cities, not included are all the small pearls that would make this list too long but are definitely worth visiting.

Sydney - the most famous and biggest city in Australia. Everybody knows Sydney, its opera house and the harbor bridge, this is one reason why many people come to Australia in the first place.

Melbourne - with its European touch it is close to what

we Europeans know about cities. Huge tourism value is created due to the old buildings and beautiful city scape.

Brisbane - is probably the most Australian city of them all, now the third largest city, it is constantly growing and renewing itself. It's beautiful parks, Southbank and general focus on shopping and lifestyle make Brisbane worth a visit.

Alice Springs - is a tiny town in the centre of Australia. It is far from all other civilisation and the perfect spot to go and see Ayers Rock and the desert. You can reach Alice Springs by plane, bus, car and train.

Canberra - is the almost unknown capital of Australia. This is where all politics and government take place.

Cairns - a small town that is mainly focused on tourism and backpackers. The rainforest is close and the weather is always very humid and warm. From Cairns it is just a few minutes to the Great Barrier Reef.

Perth - is the largest city in Western Australia and one of the most expensive ones in the world. With ridiculously high living standards due its wealth from the mining industry it is definitely worth a visit.

Take a course

Australia is a great place to take a course and get a certificate that is otherwise too expensive or hard to get.

Surf Course - probably the most famous one. It can be taken almost anywhere along the coast and is offered in a wide variety, from weekend courses to week long courses which include accommodation, food and lessons. This is a great way to meet new people and learn to surf. On the other hand, hostels close to a beach usually offer free surfboards for you to try on your own.

Farm Course - if you have no clue about farming, riding a horse or a motorbike and how to handle life stock, a farm course might be a way to get some experience which can result in a job. These courses are expensive, AU$700+ for one week, but some offer a job guarantee afterwards.

Get a Driver's License - if you don't have one yet this might be a fast and cheap way to get one. Before doing it, you should check with your department of transportation if they transfer this kind of license.

Get a Boat License - you can join a crew on a boat trip with hands on experience or even get a complete boat license. There are plenty of spots to do that.

Get a Truck License - if you want to work in a mine or

on a farm, a truck license can greatly improve your chances. They are not as expensive as in Europe and can be acquired quite fast.

Get a Forklift Licence in combination with a White Card - this can be done as a week long course for about AU$200 and makes it much easier to get a job in a related field.

Take a Parachute Course - skydiving is offered almost everywhere in Australia and it is tremendous fun and adrenaline. But if that isn't enough for you, you can take a parachute course so you can make single jumps without an instructor.

Get a Scuba License - scuba diving is wide spread all over Australia and it is a fantastic way to experience the Great Barrier Reef. If you want to dive on your own or just want a license, it can be acquired in almost any city in just 2 or 3 days.

The sky is the limit, you can learn anything while in Australia!

Travel routes

If you have no idea or just need a bit of creative input, here are some famous and frequent routes used by other travellers. Use this as a starting point on which you can build your own unique adventure.

East Coast Trip - Sydney to Cairns

Distance: 2.800 km

Duration: 20 days +

Stops: Sydney (Blue Mountains) - Byron Bay -Brisbane
- Hervey Bay (Fraser Island) - Airlie Beach (Whitsun-
days) - Townsville (Magnetic Island) - Cairns (Great
Barrier Reef)

This is probably the most popular route for back-pack-
ers and normal tourists alike. It covers all the well-
known places with a lot of famous sights and can be
done by bus, car, train and plane.

Western Australia - Perth to Darwin

Distance: 8.300 km

Duration: 2 - 8 weeks

Stops: Perth - Geraldton - Port Hedland - Broome - Darwin

If you're looking for solitude and want to see the beauty of Australian nature, this is the trip for you. It is not about how fast you can drive the distance, but about conquering vast spaces and experiencing the real Australia. On this journey you will meet almost no people, cars or petrol stations, so be prepared. The space between the cities is more important and worthwhile.

Red Centre - Adelaide to Alice Springs to Darwin
Distance: 3.000 km
Duration: 7 - 14 days
Stops: Adelaide - Coober Pedy - Ayers Rock (Uluru) -
Alice Springs - Katherine - Darwin

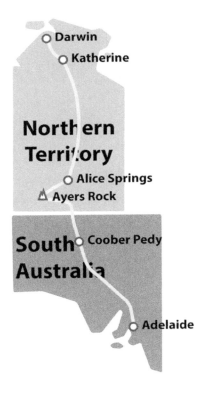

This trip lets you experience the centre of Australia, including the famous Ayers Rock. You can do this trip either by yourself or with a prearranged tour.

Rural NSW

Distance: 2.400 km / Duration: 5 - 10 days

Stops: Sydney - Canberra - Griffith - Lake Cargelligo - Dubbo - Moree - Coffs Harbour - New Castle

If you have little time, this tour might be for you. It gives you the chance to experience the beauty of rural Australia and its large agricultural sector. This trip is best done by car. The nights can be spent in local pub hotels or camping sides.

Quick Tour – Sydney to Melbourne
Distance: 900 km
Duration: 2 days
Stops: Sydney - Melbourne

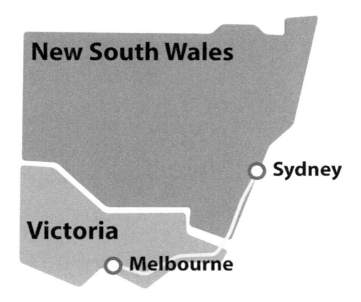

If you want to get in the mood or just want to see another city you can start with this little road trip from Sydney to Melbourne or vice versa. It takes just 2 days
when you take it slow and it can be done by all means
of transport like car, bus and train. Maybe you can find
some people and share a ride.

Tasmania
Distance: 1500 km
Duration: 7 days
Stops: Hobart - Nature – Devonport

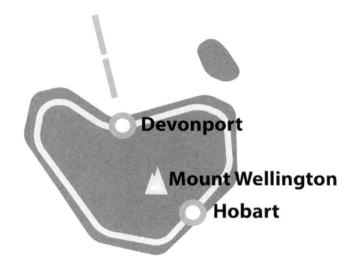

Many people forget Tasmania altogether, but it is one of the most beautiful regions in Australia and offers nature and the charm of a small island. You can reach Tasmania via ferry from Melbourne or via plane. Go and see it.

The Great Ocean Road

Distance: 350 km

Duration: 1 to 2 days

Stops: Melbourne - Torquay - Apollo Bay - The Twelve Apostles - Port Campbell - Warrnambool

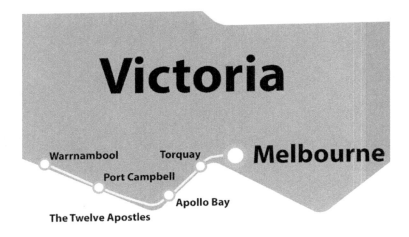

The Great Ocean Road is probably one of the most famous and beautiful drives in the world. Starting from Melbourne you follow down the coast and make several stop overs at famous towns and sights. The highlight of this trip are the Twelve Apostles near Port Campbell.

South WA - Margaret River
Distance: 400 km
Duration: 1 week
Stops: Perth - Margaret River - Augusta

The drive down from Perth to Augusta offers you the possibility to travel along the coast and experience magnificent beaches the famous wine region and is terrific for surfing. It is best done with some friends and your own or rented car. You can sleep on the beach and enjoy some solitude with frequent stopovers at the local communities.

The BIG ONE - Round Trip

Distance: 15.000 km +

Duration: 2 - 4 months

If you do this, you're the king of all road trips. After it, you know almost every corner of Australia and have seen more than other backpackers, tourists or even locals ever will. This is the holy grail of road trips and should be done with some friends and plenty of preparation.

Nightlife

You feel like a night out and want to experience the Australian nightlife? Here are a few suggestions what you can do.

Clubs - Can be found in all large tourism centres and are open all week long so you never run out of party. You will meet many new people and have a lot of fun.

Famous Clubs:
- Down Under Bar - Brisbane
- Gilligan's - Cairns
- The Emerson - Melbourne
- Scu Bar - Sydney

Festivals - Australia has many different festivals during the year which are worth visiting. They range from cultural to music festival and it is good practice to check beforehand what is happening at your destination, you might want to get some tickets or maybe all hostels are booked.

Famous festivals:
- Vivid Sydney - May to June - Sydney (light festival)
- Perth International Arts Festival - February to March - Perth
- Melbourne Food & Wine Festival - February to March - Melbourne

- Tropfestf - December – Sydney (short film festival)
- Woodford Folk Festival - December - January - Queensland
- Splendour in the Grass - July - Byron Bay (music festival)
- Ekka Royal Queensland Show - August – Brisbane (agricultural show)

Bars and Pubs - No matter how small the town, there is always at least 1 pub. They offer drinks, food and musical entertainment and are more fun when visited in rural areas where you will meet many awesome locals.

Shops - Most shops are closed at night, with exception of 7-Eleven and Petrol stations. Large discounters close between 9pm and 12pm during the week.

Activities - If you're in a rural area or on a road trip far away from large cities this is the chance to watch the stars and enjoy the silence. Just lie on the ground and watch this magnificent wonder in the sky. You can take incredible pictures due to the lack of light pollution.

Getting around

Car - A great way to travel and to see the country is by car. Either rented or bought. It gives you a whole new level of independence, but it is best to team up with other people and split the costs for fuel and rental. Most rental companies hire to people from 18 years and above.

Backpacker car and van rentals:
- Jucy - www.jucy.com.au
- Wicked Campers - www.wickedcampers.com.au

You might want to check out the standard rental companies as well, but they charge extra for drivers under 25:
- Budget - www.budget.com.au
- Avis - www.avis.com.au
- Hertz - www.hertz.com.au

When buying a car for yourself or with some friends, the notice board in a hostel is a good place to start looking. Other travellers want to sell their cars and the prices can always be negotiated. Most used cars and vans are sold with camping equipment.
Also look at www.gumtree.com.au.
Let the car get checked by a professional mechanic to make sure everything is in working condition, the money is well spend and will ensure you a working vehicle.

Bus - The most common and one of the cheapest ways of covering large distances is by bus.

The 2 big bus companies:
- Greyhound Australia - www.greyhound.com.au
- Premier Motor Service - www.premierms.com.au

They mostly serve the east coast and have a wide network of stops in almost any town or city. The bus service is usually comprised of free Wi-Fi, toilets and air conditioning. Greyhound has more comfort and more stops but Premier Motor Service is a bit cheaper. Both services must be booked in advance over the internet or travel desk and depart multiple times a day to many different locations all over Australia.

When staying in a large city for a while, consider buying a **smart** or **go card.** They offer quite substantial discounts when using the local bus and train system. These cards can be bought in news agencies and train stations.

If you have to travel really long distances go by plane, because a 23h bus ride is not comfortable, no matter how good the bus is.

Planes - Australia is a giant country where it is convenient to travel by plane for some journeys. Domestic air travel is wide spread and very cheap. Flights can be bought for under AU$100 just one or two days in advance and you save a lot of time while traveling comfortably at the same time.

Cheap domestic Airlines:
- Qantas - www.qantas.com.au
- JetStar - www.jetstar.com
- TigerAir - www.tigerair.com
- Virgin Australia - www.virginaustralia.com

Cheap flight search engines:
- IwantThatFlight - www.iwantthatflight.com.au (finds all the cheapest flights)
- TripAdvisor - www.tripadvisor.com.au

Trains - Another great way to see the country is via train. They are more expensive than other methods of transport but offer more comfort on long trips and are serviced very well. Trains leave from every major city to every major city and in-between. You can go up the east coast by train, or head to Perth, crossing the whole country.

The public train system in big cities is modern and up to date, trains run all the time and delays can be checked immediately.

Local train and bus connections:
- for Queensland - www.translink.com.au
- for New South Wales - www.nswtrainlink.info
- for Western Australia - www.transperth.wa.gov.au
- for Victoria - www.ptv.vic.gov.au

Cross country trains:

- The Great Southern Rail - www.greatsouthern-rail.com.au
- Overview of all Connections - www.rail-maps.com.au

CHAPTER 6: Work

If you're on a Working Holiday visa, you want to get a job to support your travels and lifestyle.

What kind of work

Australia offers you infinite possibilities when it comes to choosing a profession. Anything can be done here as the country has a diverse range of industries.

The three largest are:
- Mining
- Farming
- Tourism

In these fields it's generally easy to get some kind of job as they need a large workforce. When having special skills that might elevate you above the normal backpacker, try to find something in your area of expertise. If you are a mechanic, a programmer, a photographer, a sports coach or a ski expert, go for it.

You can find a job.

In order to work as a doctor or a nurse you need to take a special health examination before coming to Australia.

Backpacking jobs

A lot of travellers complain, that they can't find a job. Of course no one is walking up to you and is handing you one, although it has happened. You still have to actively write resumes, call people and look for jobs. With some effort you will definitely score something, sooner or later, so don't be disappointed if it doesn't work out in the first month.

Don't give up.

Common areas of backpacker work:
- Farm work - tractor driver, harvest, machine operator, mechanic, irrigation, cook, livestock, truck driver
- Restaurants - waiter, cook, kitchen hand, dish washer, bartender
- Mining - cook, truck driver
- Tourism - travel guide, hostel staff, cleaner
- Promotion - conventions, street sales, not for profit, events
- Seasonal Work - fruit picking, farming, tourism

- Retail - supermarkets, shopping centres, department stores
- Entertainment - Film and TV, Actor, Photographer, Musician, Model

Start looking as early as possible for something. Many jobs require you to work long hours, sometimes in very hot weather conditions, so be prepared to do such work and to go out of your comfort zone. During busy time periods on farms you usually work 12h+ a day.
When looking for a job try to search for specific keywords that fit the job you like.

Search for terms like:
- Training provided
- No experience required
- 3 - 6 months
- Short term
- Travellers welcome
- Backpacker job

Cards and certificates

Some jobs require you to take a special course before you apply. Usually they are done online and a card or certificate is sent to you via mail.

Important certifications:
- Blue Card - working with children

- White Card - construction
- RSA Certificate - Responsible Service of Alcohol

Keep in mind that different states have different requirements which means you have to do the course again if you want to work in another state. Also the names for the certificates might vary by state. Job advertisements usually specifies the needed card.

During my time I never needed a card!

Resume basics

In more than 27 months I never used my resume. If you find a job you like and that fits your skills, just **call** the employer. Talking directly to a person cuts a lot of corners and can secure you the job in a few minutes. No one wants to read 100 resumes, people like to talk.

Talk to People!

For most of the applications and e-mails sent, you won't get a reply, don't be discouraged by it. Your Curriculum Vitae (CV) or resume itself should be about 2 pages long and kept simple, no fancy fonts as it must be easy to read. Keep the language as simple as possible and try to tailor your resume to the job you are applying for, by highlighting certain skills or tasks.

Include the following things:
- Name, Address, Phone Number, E-Mail Address
- Career objective - what you're looking for
- You Skills - what you're good at
- Your employment history with the company name, the time you worked there, your position and your duties
- Internships you took
- Your education and special certificates like a driver's license, scuba license etc.
- All languages you speak and how experienced you are
- Your interests and hobbies
- Your computer skills
- If you have some, add Referees, people like your former employer that can be called and questioned about you

You can choose your own interesting resume design or just stick with the ugly one provided on the next pages.

Thomas Smith
George Street 630
LVL 4 Sydney NSW 2000
0426632515
Tom.Smith@gmail.com

CAREER OBJECTIVE
I am currently seeking casual, part time or full time employment within a progressive organisation where I can put my skills and experience to profitable use while developing both professionally and personally.

I am able to start working immediately and I am available Monday to Sunday day and night.
My working holiday visa allows me to work up to 6 months for the same employer.

SKILL SUMMARY
- Excellent communication skills
- Responsible and well organised
- Able to work autonomously or in a team environment
- Friendly but professional
- Attention to detail
- Flexible and adaptable
- Honest, punctual and reliable
- Excellent presentation
- Hard working and fast learning
- Ability to work under pressure
- Enthusiastic and positive minded
- Excellent interpersonal skills

EMPLOYMENT HISTORY
Biomedical AG, Berlin, Germany, July 2011 - September 2011
Mechanic
- mounting machines
- packing machines

Milling GmbH, Berlin, Germany, Part Time, 2007 - 2011
Industrial Mechanic
- control CNC milling machines
- finishing touch on CNC products

INTERNSHIPS
Blue Bank Berlin, Berlin, Germany, June 2007
Internship as Teller
- clients support
- banking tasks

VW Berlin, Berlin, Germany, July 2008
Internships as Mechanic
- basic mechanical tasks
- emergency car service

EDUCATION DETAILS & CERTIFICATES
Sep 2009 - Jun 2011

General Qualification for University with focus on Engineering - Goethe High School,
Berlin, Germany

Jun 2009 - Sep 2003
German Secondary School certificate - Heinrich Hertz School, Berlin, Germany

Aug 2011
International Driver License

LANGUAGES
English: Upper intermediate
German: native speaker, Spanish: beginner

INTERESTS
Reading, Music, Meeting new people, Material Arts, Team Sports

COMPUTER SKILLS
Word, Excel, Power Point, Access, Graphic Design

REFEREES
Mr Patrick Leclerc, Work n Holiday Pty Ltd, Recruitment Specialist, T: (02) 8853 7373

Skills

Experience has shown that in many cases your employment history is not as important as your skills. Especially when you apply for a short term position your boss wants core skills you can apply to the given tasks. Most people don't think too much about the skills they put down in their resumes but they are key and should be chosen carefully.

If you mention some of the core skills:

- reliable - you do what you say
- hard working - you're willing to walk the extra mile to get things done
- punctual - 9 o'clock means 8:50
- honest - I speak the truth

Make sure they apply to you.

In order to make your resume stand out choose your own particular skills, like some that can be applied to the job you're applying for. If you worked nightshift at a petrol station back home, a night job at a 7-Eleven might be something for you, if you know your way around cars and machines this is a valuable skill. With each job you acquire new skills that help you climb the ladder. The next job will be better and easier to get.

Average income

Depending on the industry, you can earn between,

AU$18.00 and AU$35.00 per hour.

These are just average estimates as there are jobs that pay less and jobs that pay way more than that. The trick is to save as much as possible so you can travel a lot afterwards. When working and living in a city, life is obviously more expensive. You have to pay for accommodation, transport, food and leisure. On the other hand, when working on a farm for example, you can save almost everything. In most cases you get free accommodation and sometimes free food and shifts are 12 hours a day, seven days a week during busy periods. Meaning there is no time to spend any money, leaving you with a soaring account.

When applying for a job make sure they pay per hour and not in a quantity unit. Fruit picking is often rewarded that way and the quotes are hard to achieve, getting paid every hour is much more rewarding and relaxing.

Best paying jobs

Mining made Australia rich, including its workers and it is currently the best paying industry. Today it is not as easy to get in to, as it was some years ago. Required skills have risen in complexity but people still get jobs in mines.

An average entry level job brings home AU$100.000 annually and includes meals, accommodation and flights to your work. Most of these jobs are organised in a two week FiFo (Fly in Fly out) roster. Two weeks' work, two weeks off. As a backpacker it makes sense to look for jobs related to the mining industry like kitchen hand and cleaning jobs.

Farming is much easier to get in to as it requires less to no experience and a lot of low skilled jobs are available. Make sure not to confuse farm work with fruit picking, farming includes: tractor driving, seeding, machine work, spraying, mechanical work, life stock, etc. If you're a mechanic or farmer in your home country, you already have a save job in Australia. These jobs pay between AU$35.000 and AU$70.000 a year.

Sometimes the rewards can be more than a pay check. Jobs can offer you exclusive advantages and perks. Working on a tourist sailing ship is one example. Try to find the compensation that fits you best, yes money is always a good thing, but experience, new skills and amazing adventures might be more important.

Where to find jobs

You can find jobs everywhere. During the harvest seasons you can find a lot of jobs in rural areas, but every city offers plenty of jobs as well. You should start looking at the job desk or black board in your hostel, they often list jobs for fruit picking or promotional work.

Another way is to walk around and look for advertisements in windows of restaurants and bars.

Knowing people is a good way of finding a job.

You might know someone in your hostel who is leaving his current job and might need a replacement. But in our modern day and age most jobs are posted online, this makes it much easier to find remote employment on farms and other rural opportunities all over Australia.

Jobs online

One site, probably the most important site in the whole of Australia is www.gumtree.com.au. It helped me with almost every job. They advertise any kind of job and offer a lot of farm and fruit picking work, the backpacker destination number one.

Other very famous sites are:
- National Harvest Telephone Information Service 1800 062 332 - www.jobsearch.gov.au/harvesttrail/
- Seek - Australia's largest professional job site - www.seek.com.au
- Job Search - www.jobsearch.gov.au
- Career One - www.careerone.com.au
- TNT Jobs - www.tntjobs.com.au
- Jobs 4 Travellers - www.jobs4travellers.com.au
- AussiJobs- http://www.aussijobs.com.au

If you have relevant skills, you can apply at an agency that will match your experience with available work and bring jobs your way. This makes sense when you have skills that are in demand or if you have worked in similar jobs in Australia before.

Seasonal harvest work

Probably the easiest way to get into a job and into farming in general is by doing harvest work during one of the many seasons. Different crops have different seasons in different parts of Australia. The government releases a new version of the Harvest Guide every year. It shows you where and when the harvest of a certain crops takes place. Make sure to call the National Harvest Telephone Information Service 1800 062 332 to get the latest information about seasonal work. Most of these jobs contribute to your 2nd years visa.

Get your free copy of the Harvest Guide here:
- https://jobsearch.gov.au/harvesttrail/

CHAPTER 7: Money

Living costs

After being in Australia for a few days you might be shocked about how expensive everything is, from food over beer to accommodation. No need to worry, this is absolutely normal because the Australian Dollar has a different value. In short, if you earn money in Australia and spend it locally it is the same as earning money in your country and spending it there. Of course some places are more expensive, cities in general and Perth and Sydney in particular. You can live much lower or much higher but while working you will earn money and spend less.

When travelling without the intention to work, pre plan and pre calculate your trip so you know roughly how much you will spend and don't get surprised by the high costs.

You can live for AU$50 or less a day as a traveller.

Travel costs

This is the place to spend your hard earned money and to have some awesome experiences. Some things you always need while travelling.

For example:
- Hostels
- Bus tickets
- Plane tickets
- Tours
- Courses

This and other small things you need on a daily bases add up quickly and it is a good idea to keep track of your spending. By not doing that I ended up almost complete blank more than once.

Becoming a member of a hostel chain can save you money and there are bus passes available that let you travel the whole east coast, hop on hop off, for around AU$420.

Expensive things

There are certain things that are expensive and that will eat your budget. Decide if you want to use them regularly.

For example, but not limited to:
- Living in a city

- Alcohol
- Parties and clubs
- Eating in restaurants
- Hotels
- Rental cars
- Chocolate
- Taxis

I encourage you to do all of these things but just not all the time, or if you have the money do them as often as you like. But trying to live with a small set budget feels very independent and freeing.

A year in numbers

This chart shows how much money I spend in my first year and how the overall finances worked out including income.

Australia 2011 – 2012 expenses and income

Accommodation		
10 weeks YHA hostels á	AU$295,00	AU$2950,00
3 weeks hostel Cairns á	AU$100,00	AU$300,00
2 weeks camper van á	AU$245,00	AU$490,00
6 months work accommodation	AU$0,00	AU$0,00
2 months staying with a friend	AU$0,00	AU$0,00
1 week work accommodation	AU$0,00	AU$0,00
Travel		
3 domestic flights	AU$100,00	AU$300,00

8 bus trips	AU$100,00	AU$800,00
Public transportation		AU$180,00
Trips		AU$1440,00
Nightlife		AU$2200,00
Shopping		
Work clothes		AU$200,00
Normal clothes		AU$600,00
Food while working, per day	AU$10,00	AU$1825,00
Food while travelling, per day	AU$18,00	AU$3276,00
Work		
Total earnings		AU$21160,00
Tax return		AU$3500,00
Total expenses		AU$14561,00
Total income		AU$24660,00
Total +		**AU$10099,00**

After my return from Australia I still had AU$10.000 that helped me for quite some time while I was preparing my next trip to Australia. I kept the money in my Australian bank account and accessed it with my debit card, credit card and PayPal account during my time overseas. When traveling to other countries inform your bank about it so they don't suspect that your card has been stolen and lock your bank account.

How to save money

While spending money on travelling or some audacious stunts you need to cut down somewhere else. The tips below show you a few areas but I'm sure you can find many more.

Cook yourself - going out for lunch and dinner is always expensive, not just in Australia. Try to cook yourself, it doesn't have to be fancy. Noodles and tomato sauce will be a good start and can cost less than a dollar. Cooking is also another helpful skill learned.

Book hostel deals - most hostels offer special discounts when you stay for a set period of time, pay for 6 nights and stay for 7 for example. If not advertised, ask if discounts or memberships are available.

Stay not in a hotel or hostel - living this way is always more expensive. Try to find another way of living, camping, traveling or working.

Sleep in your car - if you own a car it can save you a great deal of money as it is not just for transport but can also serve as accommodation. This is especially great if you're broke.

Buy discounts - supermarkets always offer an off brand version of most products. A whole range of discounts is available every day like: "Get 2 for 1", expiring soon, etc.

Travel with other people - when traveling with others you can save money by splitting the food and petrol costs and might get a group discount for certain things.

Goon - might not solve all your problems but it is cheap. Served in boxes of three to five litres that cost between AU$10 and AU$15. If you go out for a wild night, buy a pack and get drunk beforehand.

Plan and book in advance - when booking your hostel stays, plane tickets, bus rides and tours in advance you get them cheaper and don't have to worry about not finding anything.

Every dollar you save is a dollar you earn!

Taxes

If you work 6 months for the same employer, you will be treated like an Australian resident for tax purposes. Which gives you the chance to get more money back from your return and get a lower tax rate.

The rate is determined by your employer. Just pay attention when filing your tax return to provide all important information.

- Tax rate information: www.ato.gov.au/Rates/Individual-income-tax-rates/
- If you have trouble determining if you're an Australian resident for tax purposes: http://calculators.ato.gov.au/scripts/axos/axos.asp?CONTEXT=&KBS=Resident.XR4&go=ok
- Here you can calculate your taxes:

www.ato.gov.au/Calculators-and-tools/Tax-with-held-calculator/Individual-Non-business-Calcula-tor.aspx

Tax rates vary from 0 - 45%, depending on your job and income.

Tax return

While working you pay taxes, like everyone else. But there is one significant difference. As a temporary resident can get a lot of it back. AU$1000 to AU$5000 on average. The tax year ends on the 30. June, after this date you have to lodge your return, until the 31. October. Not lodging a tax return can result in penalty payments, the longer you wait the higher the fines get. You can lodge your return online or in paper form (you get the required forms in a News Agency) or with a tax organisation. All 3 ways are easy to do but a tax organisation is the most convenient. They are very quick, reliable and charge either a flat fee or a percentage of your return. Consider that a flat fee, in most cases, is the better deal. They also let you know how much you get back before it is lodged.

The tax return takes 2 - 3 weeks.

The Australian Taxation Office – ATO, provides more information here: https://www.ato.gov.au/Individuals/Lodging-your-tax-return/

Tax back organisations:

- Tax Refund 4 Travellers - www.taxrefund4travel-
  lers.com.au - flat fee AU$195
- Taxback - www.taxback.com.au - 2-3% of your
  return

To apply for your tax return, you need your TFN, the
pay slip summary or group certificate and in some
cases your pay slips. Every financial year your employer will send you a pay slip summary or group certificate summarising your income and taxes paid. Make
sure to stay in contact with him to get this information.
Some still mail it but a lot of employers changed to e-
mail which is more convenient for everybody.

Superannuation

In order to get a job, you need a Superannuation Fund.
Which is a retirement fund where your employer pays
money to, on quarterly bases. Even if you are not a per-
manent resident you need one. You can get some of
the money back after you returned from Australia and
don't consider going back. But there is a fee of roughly
50% of what is in the fund. You will receive the other
half which will be sent to your Australian or overseas
bank account. I recommend that you open one right
away, that way it is easier for you to keep track of the
money. If not, your employer will open one for you and

it can happen that you end up with more than one account in the end. When you open a superannuation account with your bank, you always have an easy online overview over all the funds. Other funds are a little harder to keep track of.

Most of them come with preinstalled insurances, get rid of them. They just cost heaps of money and aren't helping you as a temporary resident.

This link leads to the Commonwealth Bank superannuation fund **Essential Super**, which I recommend:

- https://www.commbank.com.au/personal/super-annuation/essential-super.html

The, Departing Australia Superannuation Payment, allows you to claim your money back after returning from Australia:

- https://applicant.tr.super.ato.gov.au/applicants/default.aspx?pid=1

After you issue your claim, it takes about 4 weeks to get the money.

Moving money

How do you transfer money from your overseas bank account to your Australian account and vice versa?

To Australia:
- Bring a lot of cash with you

- Use TransferWise – https://transferwise.com
- Transfer it via online banking
- Withdraw money at an ATM and deposit it into your new account
- Use a transfer service like Western Union - https://www.westernunion.com.au

From Australia:
- Take a lot of cash with you
- Use TransferWise – https://transferwise.com
- Withdraw with your Australian bank card in your home country
- Transfer to your home account via online banking
- Use a transfer service

Charges apply to all of these methods, make sure to check them out before doing anything. I advise you to keep your Australian bank account after you return, you never know.

CHAPTER 8: The first week

The first week is very important. Use the time to apply for your accounts, get settled and if you're just on holiday make your first trips and do some planning.

Get started

During this time is important to get your documents sorted.

Get:
- a sim card
- a bank account
- a superannuation fund
- a tax file number

If you did all this or if you're just on vacation, take care of:
- Extending your hostel or hotel booking
- Booking further accommodation
- Seeing the city

- Go to parties and meeting new people

You will make new friends and find new opportunities for travel as soon as you start to interact with this wonderful world around you. If you have run all your errands, it's time to make some long term plans.

What to do

After arriving you will feel a bit dizzy and tired due to your jet lack. Get used to it with a daily routine that includes getting up in the morning and going to bed at night. If you're here long term, it is time to make some plans. If you're just here for a few weeks it is key to not waste any time and see as much as possible.

Make up your mind about:
- Where you want to travel
- What you want to see
- How you want to travel
- How much time you want to spend traveling and how much working

Keep it simple and relax.

CHAPTER 9: The first month

After your first month you should be acclimated to Australia. This is the perfect time to plan for the long run.

Travel plans

Seeing the world and traveling are your main goals, I hope. You should have prepared a rough plan before coming to Australia, but now is the time to make that plan a reality.

Stuff to do:
- Make a list of all the locations you want to visit
- Book flights
- Book hostels
- Book trips

After booking all your trips you just have to follow them step by step. As mentioned earlier you can visit a travel agent to book trips and get some tips and inspiration.

Work plans

When staying for a long time you probably need to earn some cash. Plan it.

Think about:
- When you want to work
- How long you want to work
- What kind of work you want to do
- Where you want to work
- What you expect from the job
- How to find a job
- If the season is right for your kind of job

Begin applying sooner rather than later, sometimes it takes a while to get a job as competition through other travellers is large.

Money plans

After living in Australia for a while you can make accurate spending plans.

Consider:
- How long it will last
- In what ways do you save money
- When new money is coming in
- How much your journey will cost
- If you are required to pay monthly instalments of some sort

- If you have to pay important things like accommodation

Running out of money is a bad thing but it is not the end. There is always a way to find some work, live on the very cheap and make it somehow.

Don't be surprised

All these plans within plans sound boring. You might get a job earlier, might meet new people and want to travel to a completely different location. Nothing is written in stone, everything is always moving and changing. Don't be too sad about it and let the plans go. Do what you love and just follow the flow.

This is Australia, worry about things later.

CHAPTER 10: Second year

Time goes fast, especially when having the time of your life. You can't get enough and want to get your second Work & Holiday visa?

How to qualify

The second year visa gives you the chance to extend your stay in Australia for another 12 months. You can get the visa straight after your first year and don't even have to leave the country. Or you keep it for the future, as long you're under 31 when entering the country again. In order to qualify for the visa, you need three months (88 days) of regional work.

This can include, but is not limited to:
- Plant and animal cultivation
- Fishing and pearling
- Tree farming and felling
- Mining

- Construction
- etc.

You can work for as many employers as you like to collect these days. For further details and exact requirements including the eligible post codes and work types, check out the official visa page:

- http://www.border.gov.au/Trav/Visa-1/417-

How to get it

It is very simple to get. Just apply for it the same way as you did for your first year visa. This time you have to provide the name and Australian Business Number (ABN) of your employers where you worked. You can apply for the visa from outside or inside the country and must be either inside or outside when it is granted.

The application takes up to 21 days.

When extending your stay, you are able to work for the same employer for another 6 months. Everything that happened in the first year does not count anymore and don't forget to extend your health insurance and reschedule your return flight.

CHAPTER 11: Post Australia

When your time in Australia draws to an end, be it after a few weeks, a year or longer you might ask yourself what to do next.

Travel some more

If you're still hungry for travel, I encourage you to go on. Who knows when you will get that chance again. There is plenty more to see.

More countries offer Work & Travel visas:
- New Zealand
- Canada

Maybe you just want to travel. There are so many countries around Australia that can be reached fast, cheap and with little visa requirements.

Popular destinations are:
- New Zealand

- Canada
- Cambodia
- Indonesia
- India
- United Arab Emirates
- Philippines
- South Korea
- Hong Kong
- China
- Japan
- Thailand
- Singapore
- Vietnam
- USA

With about 200 other countries in world there is still plenty that wants to be discovered. Let's go.

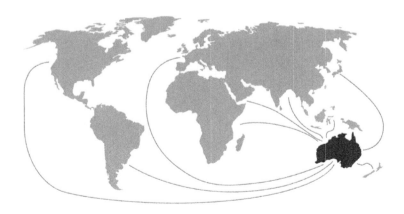

Second year

As seen in the previous chapter, it is quite easy to obtain your 2nd year visa. If you don't really know what to do next but enjoyed Australia, I suggest you stay. You get the chance to see more, work more and have more awesome adventures. Or you keep the visa for the future, like a little treasure that wants to be redeemed at some point.

It is definitely worth considering it.

Study

Maybe this was just your gap year before going to university. If you still feel that way after returning, do it. But you're now much more open to the world and maybe need something more challenging. No matter what you do, do it because you love it and always calculate the rest of the world into your plan. Going to university might give you the chance to return to Australia for an overseas semester on a student visa.

Study something important!

Work

If this trip was just a short vacation it most likely means you have to go back to your daily routine with established structures. That is perfectly fine, if you like your job. If not, this is the time to consider a change. Get a new job, travel some more, find something you love to do.

Not everybody is made for 9 to 5.

CHAPTER 12: Links

This chapter contains all the links and websites mentioned in the preceding chapters and some more. Feel free to browse all the sites and get familiar with them.

General sites

The following sites will help you in more than one situation

- Gumtree - http://www.gumtree.com.au (helps in almost any situation)
- TripAdvisor - http://www.tripadvisor.com.au
- Expedia - http://www.expedia.com.au
- The Australian Government Immigration Office - http://www.border.gov.au
- Google Drive - https://www.google.com.au/drive/
- Drop Box - www.dropbox.com
- Weather - http://www.bom.gov.au
- Ebay - www.ebay.com.au

2nd Year
- Requirements - http://www.bor-
  der.gov.au/Trav/Visa-1/417-

Travel

Travel agencies
- Peterpans - http://www.peterpans.com.au
- YHA Travel - www.yha.com.au/travel-and-
  tours/tours-and-activities/
- Wicked Travel - www.wickedtravel.com.au

Bus travel
- Greyhound - http://www.greyhound.com.au
- Premier Motor Service - www.premierms.com.au
- Buses for rural QLD - http://busqld.com.au
- Rural buses for QLD and NSW -
  http://www.crisps.com.au
- Public transport Victoria -
  http://www.vline.com.au/home/

Train travel
- Plan train journeys in Australia - http://www.rail-
  maps.com.au/austrail.htm
- For Queensland - www.translink.com.au
- For New South Wales - www.nswtrainlink.info
- For Western Australia -
  www.transperth.wa.gov.au
- For Victoria - www.ptv.vic.gov.au

- The Great Southern Rail - www.greatsouthern-rail.com.au
- Overview of all Connections - www.rail-maps.com.au

Flights & airlines
- IWantThatFlight - http://iwantthatflight.com.au
- Qantas - http://www.qantas.com.au
- Jetstar - http://www.jetstar.com
- Emirates - www.emirates.com
- TigerAir - www.tigerair.com
- Virgin Australia - www.virginaustralia.com

Accommodation & camping
- YHA Australia - https://www.yha.com.au
- Hostelworld - http://www.hostelworld.com
- Airbnb - https://www.airbnb.com.au
- Nomads Australia - http://nomadsworld.com
- Family Parks - www.familyparks.com.au
- Camping Australia - www.campinaus-tralia.com.au
- Wikicamps - http://wikicamps.com.au

Three hostels per city
Sydney
- Sydney Central YHA - from AU$39 a night - https://www.yha.com.au/hostels/nsw/sydney-sur-rounds/sydney-central-backpackers-hostel/
- Blue Elephant - from AU$ 23 a night -

http://www.elephantbackpacker.com.au
- Bounce Sydney - from AU$42 a night - http://www.bouncehostel.com.au

Brisbane
- Brisbane City YHA - from AU$25 a night - https://www.yha.com.au/hostels/qld/brisbane-surrounds/brisbane-backpackers-hostel/
- Chill Backpackers - from AU$29 a night - http://www.chillbackpackers.com
- X Base - from AU$23 a night - http://www.stayat-base.com/hostels/australia/brisbane/base-bris-bane-uptown

Melbourne
- Melbourne Central YHA - from AU$36 a night - https://www.yha.com.au/hostels/vic/melbourne-hostels/melbourne-central-hostel/
- Nomads Melbourne - from AU$31 a night - http://nomadsworld.com/hostels/australia/mel-bourne/nomads-melbourne
- King Street Backpackers - from AU$30 a night http://www.kingstreetbackpackers.com.au

Cairns
- Cairns Central YHA - from AU$25 a night - https://www.yha.com.au/hostels/qld/cairns-and-far-north-queensland/cairns-backpackers-hostel/

- Nomads Cairns - from AU$16 a night - http://nomadsworld.com/hostels/australia/cairns/nomads-cairns
- Gilligans - from AU$24 a night - https://www.gilligans.com.au

Adelaide
- Adelaide Central YHA - from AU$30 a night - https://www.yha.com.au/hostels/sa/adelaide/adelaide-backpackers-hostel/
- Adelaide Travellers In - from AU$26 a night - http://nomadsworld.com/hostels/australia/adelaide/adelaide-travellers-inn
- Hostel 109 - from AU$32 a night - http://www.hostel109.com/

Perth
- Perth City YHA - from AU$29 a night - https://www.yha.com.au/hostels/wa/perth-surrounds/perth-backpackers-hostel/
- Billabong Backpackers - from AU$20 a night - http://nomadsworld.com/hostels/australia/perth/billabong-backpackers
- City Perth Backpackers Hostel - from AU$24 a night - http://www.cityperthhostel.com.au/rooms/

Car and camper van hire
- Imoova - http://www.imoova.com
- Budget - www.budget.com.au

- Avis - www.avis.com.au
- Hertz - www.hertz.com.au

Visa
- Visitor visa options - http://www.border.gov.au/Trav/Visi/Visi
- Working Holiday visa (subclass 417) - http://www.border.gov.au/Trav/Visa-1/417-
- Visa pricing estimator - http://www.border.gov.au/Trav/Visa/Visa-1

Insurance
- Allianz - http://www.allianz-assistance.co.uk
- CareMed - https://www.work-and-travel-insurance.com

Mobile Carriers
- Telstra - https://www.telstra.com.au
- Optus - http://www.optus.com.au
- Vodafone - http://www.vodafone.com.au/personal
- Virgin Mobile - https://www.virginmobile.com.au

Work

Job sites
- Gumtree - http://www.gumtree.com.au
- Seek - http://www.seek.com.au
- Job search by the Government -

http://jobsearch.gov.au
- Career One - http://www.careerone.com.au
- TNT - http://www.tntjobs.com.au
- Backpacker Jobs - http://www.back-packerjobsaustralia.com.au
- Jobaroo - http://www.jobaroo.com
- Labour Solutions - http://www.laboursolu-tions.com.au
- Backpacker Job Board - http://www.back-packerjobboard.com.au
- Travelers At Work - http://www.taw.com.au
- Workstay - http://www.work-stay.com.au/Home.htm
- Backpacker Downunder- http://www.backpack-downunder.com/category/jobs
- Harvest Jobs by the Government - https://jobsearch.gov.au/harvesttrail/
- Jobs 4 Travelers - www.jobs4travellers.com.au
- AussiJobs- http://www.aussijobs.com.au

Money

Banks

- Commonwealth Bank - https://www.commbank.com.au
- Westpac Bank - http://www.westpac.com.au
- ANZ - https://www.anz.com.au
- National Australian Bank - NAB - http://www.nab.com.au

- Western Union - https://www.westernunion.com.au

Superannuation
- Commonwealth Bank Superannuation - https://www.commbank.com.au/personal/superannuation/essential-super.html

Taxes
- Australian Taxation Office - ATO - https://www.ato.gov.au
- TFN Information - https://www.ato.gov.au/individuals/tax-file-number/apply-for-a-tfn/foreign-passport-holders,-permanent-migrants-and-temporary-visitors---tfn-application/
- TFN Application - https://iar.ato.gov.au/IARWeb/default.aspx?pid=4&sid=1&outcome=1
- Tax rate information - www.ato.gov.au/Rates/Individual-income-tax-rates/
- Determine if you're an Australian resident for tax purpose - http://calculators.ato.gov.au/scripts/axos/axos.asp?CONTEXT=&KBS=Resident.XR4&go=ok
- Calculate your taxes - www.ato.gov.au/Calculators-and-tools/Tax-withheld-calculator/Individual-Non-business-Calculator.aspx

Tax Back

- http://www.taxrefund4travellers.com.au
- http://www.taxback.com.au
- https://www.ato.gov.au
- https://www.ato.gov.au/Individuals/Lodging-your-tax-return/

Superannuation Return

- https://applicant.tr.super.ato.gov.au/applicants/default.aspx?pid=1
- https://www.immi.gov.au/employers/rsms_postcodes.htm

Currency Converter

- http://finance.yahoo.com/currency-converter/

Apps

Here are some important apps for your smartphone or tablet - they all have one thing in common, they are FREE.

Just look them up in your app store (iOS or Google Play):
- The App of your Bank (every bank has an easy to use app)
- Gumtree
- Airbnb
- Hostelworld
- Google Maps
- here - Offline Maps and Navigation App
- dict.cc - dictionary
- My currency exchange rates converter
- Skype
- A weather app

Enjoy your time in Australia because this is one of the best things you can do.

Have fun.

Your travel notes

_____

_____

_____

_____

_____

_____

_____

_____

_____

_____

_____

_____

_____

_____

Printed in Great Britain
by Amazon